THE PROJECT MANAGER'S LITTLE BOOK OF CHEATS

QUICK STEPS, RELEVANT TIPS, AND APPLICABLE ADVICE TO SOLVING COMMON PROBLEMS AND QUESTIONS FOCUSED AROUND THE WORK OF A PROJECT MANAGER

BETH SPRIGGS

Table of Contents

Chapter 1: Starting   page   3
Chapter 2: Communication   page 19
Chapter 3: Change   page 39
Chapter 4: Scope   page 47
Chapter 5: Time   page 59
Chapter 6: Risk   page 69
Chapter 7: Process   page 83
Chapter 8: Portfolios   page 95
Chapter 9: Teams   page 101
Chapter 10: Tools   page 115
Chapter 11: Vendors   page 121

Table of Questions

Chapter 1 – Starting..........................page 3

1. What are some good interview questions for a project manager position?................................page 4

2. I just hired a project manager who is new to project management. What advice should I give them to get started?..page 6

3. I hear that to be an awesome project manager I need to build relationships. It seems like most people build relationships by sharing personal stuff and talking about their kids or pets. I don't like sharing personal things. How can I still build strong relationships?..page 7

4. What's the purpose of project initiation? I mean, it's not really a necessary step, right?..................page 9

5. What are the critical steps of project initiation? Now that I know I should be doing it..................page 10

6. There is confusion on who owns what in my project. What can I do?..page 12

7. Smart Start Questions: Myth or Truth?.........page 13

8. I want to become Project Management Professional (PMP) certified. How do I get started?..........page 14

9. What other certifications does the Project Management Institute (PMI) offer?................page 16

10. Where can I go to get help from others with similar issues as my own?..page 18

Chapter 2 – Communication..................page 19

11. My boss, or anybody, and I don't agree. How can we reach an understanding?......................page 20

12. I need to convince someone of my idea. How do I sell an idea?...page 22

13. How can I communicate more effectively with a virtual team?...page 23

14. I have to work with or manage someone who is poor at communicating. Is there anything I can do?..page 26

15. I'm introverted, how can I communicate effectively within my comfort zone?............................page 29

16. Since most of my work communication is through email, how can I make my email communications more effective?...page 30

17. It seems like people aren't reading my email messages. It's very frustrating. What can I do?..page 32

18. I have too many emails. What can I do?......page 35

19. Something went wrong and people are panicking! How do I calm them down and not lose their trust?..page 37

Chapter 3 – Change.........................page 39

20. What are the primary principles for effective user adoption or change management?.............page 40

21. What characteristics make for a good change agent?..page 41

22. How can I convince those who are change resistant?..................................page 42
23. What is user adoption vs. user adaptability? And why do I care?..................................page 44

Chapter 4 – Scope..........................page 47
24. What are some methods for gathering requirements?..................................page 49

25. While gathering requirements I noticed that some of them don't seem appropriate or helpful for the business objectives of the project. Some might even hurt the desired outcome. But these are the requirements provided by the customer. What should I do?..................................page 51

26. What is Expectation Inflation? And why do I care?..................................page 52

27. How can I prevent scope creep?..................page 55

28. People keep requesting specific project deliverables that require customization. Customizing is expensive, difficult to maintain, and creates risk. The more we can stick to an out-of-the-box solution the better off we'll be in the long term. How can I deter requests for customizations?..................................page 57

Chapter 5 – Time..........................page 59
29. How can I provide a quick time estimate?....page 60

30. How can I protect my project's timeline?......page 61

31. My project is behind schedule. I don't have extra resources to add and I've already paralleled all the tasks I can. The problem is that I'm waiting on people to give input or feedback and they are not

responding in a timely manner because it's not a priority for them. I don't manage them so I can't adjust their priorities. What can I do?............page 62

32. What's a Critical Path? And why do I care?..page 64

33. How can I manage my time better?.............page 66

34. How can I have a better work/life balance, without quitting my job?..page 68

Chapter 6 – Risk..............................page 69
35. What goes into a risk register?....................page 70

36. How frequently should a risk register be reviewed and updated?...page 72

37. What are some common project risks to include or consider in a risk register?...........................page 73

38. What makes an assumption so dangerous?..page 76

39. Assumptions introduce a lot of risk. What are some common assumptions to watch out for?.......page 77

40. How can I uncover assumptions people might be holding that would impact my work?.............page 78

Chapter 7 – Process........................page 83
41. How can I tell if a project is getting off track before it's too late?..page 85

42. What's the difference between Waterfall and Agile?..page 90

43. What is the Agile Manifesto?.......................page 91

44. What is this thing called SCRUM? It sounds silly..page 92

45. What's the difference between process management, project management, and product management?..page 93

Chapter 8 – Portfolios........................page 95
46. What is portfolio management?....................page 96

47. What process could I use to evaluate project requests to determine if they should be approved or not?..page 97

48. What criteria could I use to prioritize approved projects?...page 98

49. How can I tell people that we won't work on their project when they want it, or possibly not at all, without ruining my relationship with them?...page 99

Chapter 9 – Teams...........................page 101
50. What are some tips on leading a virtual team?...page 103

51. How can I make my team meetings more productive?...page 104

52. What is a team promise and why should I have one?..page 105

53. What are some good, quick team building activities and icebreakers?...page 107

54. How can I keep my team motivated, and avoid burn out for myself and my team?.....................page 109

55. I have to give someone some hard feedback. What should I consider before going into the

conversation?..............................page 111

56. How do I start a conversation in which I'm giving hard feedback?............................page 113

57. How can I coach someone who needs to deliver hard feedback but is resistant because it makes them uncomfortable?................................page 114

Chapter 10 – Tools..........................page 115

58. My project tracking needs have grown beyond Microsoft Excel. What are some good project management tools?....................................page 116

59. I need to track a portfolio of projects and resources. What are some portfolio and resource management tools?...page 117

60. What are other technology tools that could help me as a project manager?................................page 118

Chapter 11 – Vendors.....................page 121

61. What are different types of requests sent to vendors?...page 122

62. Is there an alternative to a Request for Proposal (RFP)?..page 123

63. How can I foster a positive working partnership with a vendor?...page 125

64. How is vendor management changing? What trends should I be aware of?................................page 126

65. Things are taking a turn for the worse with a vendor that is critical to my project. What can I do?..page 128

For my boys

Introduction

There is no such thing as cheating in project management, but if there were it would be this book. Since 1999 I've been collecting quick steps, relevant tips, and applicable advice to solving common problems and questions focused around the work of a project manager. When you have a question or problem do you have time to stop what you're doing and read a three-hundred-page book on a single topic? Wouldn't it be great if you could open a book and find a one to two-page answer that you can apply immediately, in the moment when you need it? Lucky you! You're holding that in your hands right now.

This book has hopes and dreams. It hopes that it will sit on or in your desk and be opened frequently when questions or problems arise. It wants you to write on its pages, make your own notes, and highlight what works for you. And it dreams that you will share its contents with your colleagues.

If you have ideas for more questions, quotes, tips, or things to add to this book, I would love to hear them.
contact@bethspriggs.com

CHAPTER 1: STARTING

1. What are some good interview questions for a project manager position?

Here are a few suggestions:

1. What do you spend most of your time on as a Project Manager?

2. How would you manage communication in a multicultural environment?

3. How would you manage communication in a virtual environment?

4. Describe to me your typical day as a Project Manager. Include what activities you do and the tools you use.

5. What advice would you give someone who is brand new to project management?

6. Walk me through your process: What do you do first? Why? What do you do next? What was the result?

7. What was something you accomplished that you think someone else in your role might not have gotten done, or where you approached it differently from how others might have, or where you went above and beyond?

8. Describe a scenario of a project, and then ask, "What would make that project fail?" followed by "What would you do to prevent failure from happening?"

9. Describe another project scenario that goes something like, "Imagine you're working on a high profile project. It impacts multiple teams and customers, has significant impact for the organization's goals, costs a relatively significant amount of money, and is a twelve-month project." Then pose these two questions:

    a. You're two months away from launching and you get a phone call from the vendor you're working with, and the vendor informs you that they won't have the product ready on time. What do you do?

    b. You're two weeks away from launching and a senior staff person comes to you and says they don't think your testing has been thorough enough, they've tried testing some features and have seen issues, and they have heard about testing issues from their staff. They don't think the product is ready to launch in two weeks and should be delayed. How do you respond?

2. I just hired a project manager who is new to project management. What advice should I give them to get started?

This list of advice was collected from project managers with at least ten years of experience, from a wide variety of fields and backgrounds. Many shared the same sentiments.

- Build trust and relationships
- It's more about the relationships
- The work is very collaborative
- Listen
- Communication, communication, communication
- It's more than technical skills
- It's less about project management than it is about project leadership
- Be flexible
- There's never a cookie-cutter approach
- Rely on common sense and instinct
- You need discipline
- Stick it out - finish one project
- Your job is follow up
- Planning, planning, planning, planning
- Daily focus on top priorities
- Take responsibility and go
- Keep a sense of humor

3. I hear that to be an awesome project manager I need to build relationships. It seems like most people build relationships by sharing personal stuff and talking about their kids or pets. I don't like sharing personal things. How can I still build strong relationships?

   1. Ask someone for their advice or opinion about something on which you're working. It shows that you value their opinion and expertise. Express appreciation for their advice.

   2. Listen. Really listen. When you find your mind drifting or already crafting your reply, snap the metaphorical rubber band on your wrist, take a deep breath and listen. Ask questions about what they are saying that are still about them and not you. Most people like talking about themselves and appreciate genuine interest.

   3. Offer to help if you can.

   4. When someone shares something with you, ask them follow up questions to demonstrate your genuine interest in what they're saying.

   5. Give a shout-out to that person or people they manage. Vocalize to someone else your appreciation for something that person has done for you.

Never underestimate the value of asking experts.

Talking to people who have been there, done that can give you more insight and revelation than you ever thought possible. They will explain things about which you made assumptions.

4. What's the purpose of project initiation? I mean, it's not really a necessary step, right?

The purpose is to make sure that people's expectations line up with the purpose of the project. This means you have to clearly understand what stakeholders expect from the final outcome, that you have an initial understanding of the resources it would take to reach that outcome, and that you understand how the project connects to and furthers organizational goals. That way you know you're working on the right thing. Otherwise you're left making drastic assumptions that could get you into a lot of trouble.

Expectations = Project Purpose

5. What are the critical steps of project initiation? Now that I know I should be doing it.

STEP 1: Write up a stakeholder register. You'll use this as a starting point for your communication plan. Identify the project stakeholders and document the following.
    a. Who
    b. Their involvement or stake in the project
    c. Their roles, e.g. Project Sponsor, Experts, Contributors

STEP 2: Share the stakeholder register with the stakeholders.
    What? That's just nonsense.

    No really. Too often we write it and leave it, which is kind of pointless. It's really only useful if you share it, because in doing so you are checking your assumptions on who the stakeholders should be and what their roles are in the project.

STEP 3: Write up a project charter that includes the following.
    a. Project Statement or Description – one paragraph stating the what, why, who, and when
    b. Business Case – the purpose or justification demonstrating impact
    c. Assumptions / Constraints
    d. Goals & Success Criteria
    e. High Level:
        i. Scope
        ii. Budget
        iii. Timeline
        iv. Risk
    f. Authorization – approval to move ahead with the project

STEP 4: You guessed it... share the project charter! Let the key stakeholders see it and solicit their comments and questions. Not only will it help check assumptions you might have made, but by sharing it you start to get buy-in for your project. Who doesn't need buy-in?

6. There is confusion on who owns what in my project. What can I do?

Define ownership in partnership. When was the last time you explicitly defined what it meant for you or someone else to own a project or a piece of work? We are quick to take or assign something, then we make assumptions about what owning that thing means and we move forward without ever checking those assumptions. We should explicitly state what it means to own something. You might find that others had a different idea of what ownership meant to them.

Ownership doesn't have to be singularly defined for every project. The definition can vary depending on the work, but it should be agreed upon. The benefit comes in having a shared understanding, so there is no confusion about who is responsible for what and when. A good place to start is listing out responsibilities and indicating who is responsible for what. What other ownership traits would you add to this list?

Who is responsible for:
- Primary communication / facilitating communication
- Ensuring success measures / goals are met
- User adoption of deliverables
- Keeping work on time, within budget, within scope
- Quality of deliverables
- Creating planning documents
- Setting (or re-setting) stakeholder expectations
- Getting and understanding the full context of the work, and the implications
- Obtaining stage-gate approvals
- Execution
- Training
- Ongoing support / maintenance
- _____
- _____

7. Smart Start Questions: Myth or Truth?

The idea that there are five perfect questions you should begin every project with sounds like something of legend. Could it be true? I interviewed over fifty people who came up with over eighty questions. Most of the questions focused on timeline, scope, resources, compliance, communication, priorities, and feasibility. However, these five questions stood out as especially thoughtful questions to ask at the start of any project. Could these be the legendary "Smart Start Questions?" Not likely, but they are still worth asking!

1. **What are your pain points?**
2. **What does success look like?**
3. **Is there a previous example or precedent?**
4. **What is the buy-in?**
5. **How will this change make us act or reflect in a new way?**

What are your smart start questions?

_____

_____

_____

_____

8. I want to become Project Management Professional (PMP) certified. How do I get started?

1. Join PMI, the Project Management Institute at www.pmi.org. The certification is through them.

2. Download and read the PMP Certification handbook, found at www.pmi.org under Certifications.

3. Start filling out the application. It takes a while to document the history of hours you've spent on projects, so start working on it and fill it out over time.

4. Take whatever coursework hours you need. 35 hours of coursework are required.
    a. Register at www.ProjectManagement.com, it's free with your PMI membership and offers a lot of great learning opportunities for free credit hours.

5. Finish your application and submit it with payment. After it's accepted, schedule your testing date at least two months out. You have one year after your application is accepted to take the exam.

6. Find and sign up for an exam prep course that's between one and three weeks before your scheduled exam date, but no further out than three weeks.

7. Read the most recent PMBOK® guide, the Project Management Body of Knowledge. Really read it, don't just skim through it. Get out your highlighter, circle things, underline things, draw hearts around things, keep it by your bed at night.

8. After the exam prep course, go through an exam prep book with practice questions. Complete the whole book. Allow one full week to do this.

9. Take the test. It's a four-hour exam. Be mentally prepared to spend the full four hours taking the exam.

10. Frame your certificate and hang it proudly on your wall.

9. What other certifications does the Project Management Institute (PMI) offer?

The following is taken directly from PMI's website: www.pmi.org/certification

CAPM® Certified Associate in Project Management
For project managers who are still working toward having enough hours of experience for a PMP certification. Demonstrates your understanding of the fundamental knowledge, terminology and processes of effective project management.

PgMP® Program Management Professional
For those who manage multiple, complex projects to achieve strategic and organizational results.

PfMP® Portfolio Management Professional
Demonstrates your proven ability in the coordinated management of one or more portfolios to achieve organizational objectives.

PMI-PBA® PMI Professional in Business Analysis
Spotlights your ability to work effectively with stakeholders to define their business requirements, shape the output of projects and drive successful business outcomes.

PMI-ACP® PMI Agile Certified Practitioner
For those who believe in and apply agile principles and practices on projects. Bridges agile approaches such as SCRUM, XP, LEAN and Kanban.

PMI-RMP® PMI Risk Management Professional
Recognizes demonstrated knowledge and expertise in the specialized area of assessing and identifying project risks along with plans to mitigate threats and capitalize on opportunities.

PMI-SP® PMI Scheduling Professional
Recognizes demonstrated knowledge and advanced experience in the specialized area of developing and maintaining project schedules.

> Try not.
> Do, Or do not.
> there is no try.
> —Yoda

10. Where can I go to get help from others with similar issues as my own?

ProjectManagement.com, the online community and member to member networking site for the Project Management Institute (PMI). If you're a PMI member, you automatically have free access to projectmanagement.com. www.projectmanagement.com

Local PMI Chapters www.pmi.org/membership/chapters-pmi-chapters.aspx

Attend PMI, ProjectManagement.com, and local chapter conferences and webinars. Networking through those forums is a great way to connect with others and find help.

LinkedIn Groups: Project Management 2.0, ProjectManagementcom, PMO, I want to be a PMP

Contact@BethSpriggs.com
I'm always happy when people reach out to me directly with questions or to share things they have learned.

CHAPTER 2: COMMUNICATION

11. My boss, or anybody, and I don't agree. How can we reach an understanding?

Start by asking the other person, "Can you walk me through your thought process?" Explain that you're looking for context. You might learn new information that you didn't know before, so listen with an open mind and be willing to change your perspective based on what you hear. Either you will come around to their point of view or you now have the background to shift their thinking. Ask if you can now share where you're coming from because you want to make sure you're aligned.

Typically, we start with the same end goal in mind, and from there thought processes diverge. The further back you go in the thought process, the easier it becomes to change someone's thinking. The closer you are to the point of origination, the shared goal that started the chain of thought, the smaller the degree of difference between your thinking and someone else's. Thus the change isn't as large and it's easier to shift. The further down the chain of thought you go, the greater the distance becomes and the harder it will be to align your thinking.

By learning the other person's thought process and sharing your own, you can get closer to the point of origination and it will be easier to change either their or your thinking so you are aligned.

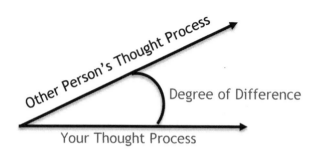

It ain't what you don't know that gets you into trouble. It's what you know for sure that just ain't so.

--Mark Twain

12. I need to convince someone of my idea. How do I sell an idea?

This secret formula has always worked for me, even with the toughest of audiences. Be sure to use specifics and details relevant to what you're selling:

a. Tell a story. Get their attention with a short story that illustrates the problem for which you're solving.

b. Share relevant statistics; specific facts and just facts. People love statistics, and facts are indisputable.

c. Explain the change you want to see, and show how that change will have an impact toward your desired outcome.

d. Apply it to your audience. Explain the direct implications to them and their work. People are self-interested and want to know what's in it for them, or what is being asked of them.

e. Provide multiple alternatives to the current way of thinking which will support your idea. You can steer toward a particular solution, but if you're able to give more than one path forward and can let the audience choose then they will be more bought in since they will have had a hand in the final decision.

13. How can I communicate more effectively with a virtual team?

Most communication with a virtual team is written. This is often due to time zone differences, scheduling conflicts, speed, ease, and comfort. However, written communication comes with a number of challenges. It can be harder to get the right message across or even get people to read. Here are some tips for communicating with virtual teams:

a. Short
Keep your messages short. Edit them.

b. Frequent
Stay connected on a regular basis. This helps with relationship building, which can also be challenging in a virtual work environment. It also creates opportunities for asking questions, getting advice, and collaboration that might not otherwise happen.

c. Varied
Switch up the communication method. Don't always default to email. Think about when it would make more sense to send a quick chat or text. If your email gets into its third or fourth paragraph, consider scheduling a video call instead. When sending a message to a group of people, send the same message through a variety of different formats; email, chat, message board, team calls, all-staff message, etc. That way it's more likely to be read by the various people in the group who have different communication preferences.

(continued on next page)

d. Deliberate
In an office you walk down the hallway or get something from the kitchen and start up a conversation by chance with someone which turns out to be super beneficial. Online, those conversations don't happen by chance, you have to make them happen. You have to deliberately reach out at either planned or unplanned times in order to create the space for the, "Hey, now that we're talking, can I ask you about...?" One way is to have regularly scheduled brief check-ins with key staff. Another is to randomly say hi over chat, email, or phone just to see how someone is doing. Don't wait for the conversation to come to you, reach out and make it happen.

*Messaging impact is 7% words; **38%** tone, volume, and pitch; and **55%** body language and facial expressions.*

Comb Your Hair & Turn On Your Camera

14. I have to work with or manage someone who is poor at communicating. Is there anything I can do?

Being on the receiving end of poor communication can feel like opening a box of LEGO's® and finding playdough. It's not what you expected, it doesn't make sense to you, and you're not sure what to do with it. You hoped for clear instructions and instead you got a shapeless lump.

Poor communicators can be super frustrating. If you manage the person, you could recommend some communication training. But in most cases we don't have that option and we don't have much, if any, influence to change someone else. But we *can change ourselves* and how we approach others. Here are a couple keys.

Understand
: Work on understanding how the other person learns, listens, and communicates. Then do what you can to adjust your communication style when interacting with that person. Empathy is key.

Ask
: If you don't understand what they are communicating, don't just walk away in frustration and blame. Ask lots of questions until you understand. Patience is key.

*The biggest
communication problem
is we do not listen
to understand.
We listen to reply.*

15. I'm introverted, how can I communicate effectively within my comfort zone?

1. Work on making your email communications really effective.

    The most comfortable way for most introverts to communicate is by email. The problem is that email isn't always the most effective way to get a message across. Refer to the next two questions (#16 and #17) for tips on writing effective emails.

2. One to two days prior to a meeting, send or ask for a detailed agenda and a list of open questions.

    A detailed agenda will give you and others the chance to prepare in advance so that the meeting can stay on track and end faster. The list of questions allows you and others to reply to the questions ahead of time, possibly creating the opportunity to cancel the meeting. I don't know about you, but I get a small rush anytime a meeting is cancelled.

3. If you need processing time, ask for it.

    Sometimes you might need extra time to think through something. Don't feel pressured to answer on the spot. If you need time to thoughtfully think through a response, simply say, "Can I have some time to process this and get back to you with a response?"

4. When possible, schedule meetings back to back

    Meetings can often run over. Scheduling back to back meetings forces a hard stop since you have to move on to your next meeting. This can reduce overall time spent in meetings.

16. Since most of my work communication is through email, how can I make my email communications more effective?

Here are some tips:

a. First write down your stream of thought to get out all your ideas, then go back and edit. Always edit. If you edit while writing out your thoughts, instead of after, you could get stuck and it's easier to lose your ideas.

b. Remove pronouns (he, she, they, it), especially "it," and vague words like "that." Using vague words leaves room for misinterpretations. For example, instead of writing, "I think that's a good idea," you would instead write, "I think Amy's idea to consolidate training materials is a good one."

c. Always re-read the first sentence of your message. Even if you don't re-read the rest of your message, at least read the first sentence to make sure it makes sense.

d. When replying, always reread your message as if the thread below it isn't there. This is a quick and effective way to make sure your message is clear.

e. When replying, change the subject as needed to keep it relevant.

f. If the email requires an action to be taken by the recipient(s), start the subject line with <action required by xxx date>, followed by the regular subject. Be sure to include the due date. That way it's obvious just from the subject that something is due and when.

g. People like consistency. Be consistent in emailing out meeting agendas and post-meeting notes. If the notes are stored in an online drive or server then you can schedule an automated email with a link to the folder so you don't have to remember to send the email, and your communications will be consistent and reliable.

h. Don't debate through email. If the thread becomes contentious or goes back and forth disagreeing, schedule a call or meeting to talk it through. You'll save a lot of time and frustration.

17. It seems like people aren't reading my email messages. It's very frustrating. What can I do?

The hard truth is, we don't read. We skim. It's scientifically proven. Through eye-tracking technology we know that people skim the text on a page in the shape of an "F".

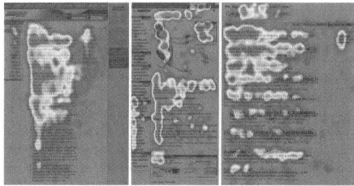

http://conversionxl.com/10-useful-findings-about-how-people-view-websites/

The following are some tips for writing emails for people who skim, which is basically everybody.

    a. Edit. I repeat... e d i t. Keep your messages short. Delete superfluous text. After you've written your message, read it and edit to make it shorter.

    b. Your first sentence should be your primary message.

    c. After you've written several sentences, switch to bullets or lists.

    d. Use memes, gifs, emojis, & emoticons. Don't shy away from these in your work communications. They will grab attention, and attention is a precious commodity.

e. If your email ends up being longer than 2-3 paragraphs, schedule a meeting to talk instead.

f. Use humor. If people expect your messages will make them laugh, they'll be more likely to read. This especially helps with long messages.

If your emails still aren't communicating as you would hope, try sending the same message through multiple mediums such as chats, posts, micro-blogs, or videos. And remember, if your message is so long that you won't bother re-reading it before sending, then don't expect anyone else to read it either.

To emoticon, or not to emoticon? That is the question.

To which I always answer yes :-) but only after you've considered two things.

1. *Culture
   and*
2. *Context*

If the culture of your work environment is agreeable to emoticons, and if the context of the message is appropriate for them, then go for it! ☺

18. I have too many emails. What can I do?

1. Use folders and filters. File emails into folders when you're done reading and responding to them, or delete the email if there's no need to keep it. Create a separate task item if the message requires you to take action. Set up rules to auto-filter emails into other folders in order to keep them organized.

2. If an email is more than three months old and still in your in-box, do you really need to keep it? If yes, then file it to a different folder. Otherwise, delete it.

3. To get at the root cause of people sending you so many emails, establish and share communication norms for how you and/or your team prefer to use different methods of communication. Purposefully restrict what email should be used for. Tailor your norms to fit your communication preferences.

   <u>Sample Communication Norms</u>
   Use the following methods for the following types of communication:
   a. Chat – for quick questions with quick answers
   b. Meeting (phone, video call, or in-person) – to talk through and discuss something in more depth
   c. Text – if it is urgent, needs immediate attention and/or it's after normal work hours
   d. Email – if you don't need an immediate response, or any response, or if time is required in order to respond (thinking time or time to complete an action)

A Conversation with a 4-Year-Old at Bedtime

Mom: Can you go to the bathroom please?

Kid: I don't have to go.

Mom: I want you to go now so you won't have to go in the middle of the night.

Kid: I won't have to go in the middle of the night.

Mom: Are you sure? I really don't want you to have to go to the bathroom in the middle of the night.

Kid: I'm sure, Mommy. I won't have to go in the middle of the night.

PAUSE

Kid: I might have to go in the front of the night or the back of the night, but not the middle.

19. Something went wrong and people are panicking! How do I calm them down and not lose their trust?

1. Talk to Your Project Sponsor
   First things first, make sure you have notified your project sponsor if they don't already know. They can help, and you don't want your sponsor to hear about the issue from someone else. It's better if they hear it from you first.

2. Express Understanding
   Before you present solutions to the issue, express to the people impacted that you understand what they are feeling. Whether their feelings are justified or not doesn't matter. What matters is that you demonstrate empathy. If you start with empathy, they will be more likely to listen to what you have to say. This could look like:
   - "I'm so sorry this is taking up your time."
   - "This situation must be very frustrating for you. Tell me your frustrations and I'll do everything I can to help."
   - "This is a rough situation and I understand the anxiety and concern this must certainly be causing."

3. Learn Their Concerns
   Next, ask some probing questions to learn what their specific concerns are about. Are they worried about the drain on their time? The success of the project? The impact to their team or other people? Ask a bunch of questions until you really understand all their concerns. If this impacts a group of people, talk to a few representatives.

4. **Explain the Cause & Present Solutions**
   Now you are ready to explain what happened and to present some solutions. The first three steps help diffuse the panic and lay a foundation that will make this step far more successful. If you need time to research the issue and solutions, still do the first three steps and then begin your research. Reassure people that you're working on it and explain your next steps.

5. **Don't Blame**
   Even if the panic was completely unfounded, resist the temptation to lay blame. Simply explain the issue and answer questions until they understand. Blaming will damage your relationship and can create distrust.
   - Stick to the facts
   - Explain the issue and solutions in simple, easy to understand language. Don't try to confuse people with complicated language.
   - Directly address their specific concerns which you learned from step three.

This will foster trust and strengthen relationships even in a bad situation.

CHAPTER 3: CHANGE

20. What are the primary principles for effective user adoption or change management?

1. Get buy-in from the top.

2. Make a formal case.
   Show the impact of the change, and call out the day-to-day implications the change will have for different levels of staff or customers.

3. Identify change agents.
   Ask change agents to cheerlead, be early adopters, give feedback, and help train.

4. Complete a change tolerance assessment.
   Focus on understanding the culture of your company or customers and how the culture influences change acceptance.

5. Demonstrate value.
   Show the users what's in it for them.

6. Address fears.
   Uncover any fears the change might be causing. See question 22 on how to help those who are change resistant.

7. Use humor.
   I know I say that a lot in this book, but it works!

21. What characteristics make for a good change agent?

Finding someone with all of these traits would be exceptional. If you find someone with a majority of these traits, they would make a great change agent for your project.

a. Values differences
b. Leads by example, is a role model
c. Is inclusive and transparent
d. Mindful of own biases, is self-aware
e. Coaches others
f. Solves problems
g. Breaks through silos, encourages collaboration
h. Lives and honors the company's core values

22. How can I convince those who are change resistant?

What is your phobia? Are you afraid of heights? Spiders? Snakes? Think about how that thing makes you feel. You fear something bad will happen to you. Now consider people who are change resistant. They are afraid that the change will result in something bad happening to them. The change could feel threatening to their job responsibilities, or something over which they feel personal ownership. They could be afraid of being asked to learn something new which they don't believe they can understand. Or they don't have spare time to learn anything new. Here are some ways to convince those who are change resistant to adapt to your change.

   a. Excitement
   Build excitement and anticipation around the thing you're rolling out. You could do a weekly countdown and include one or two ways in which their work will be made easier. Send out a vague teaser message, like a representative image with a note, "Its coming." Get a couple people excited and ask them to talk about it with others to create a buzz. Use social media, chat, and blogs to start spreading the word. Add some humor to make it engaging!

   b. Need
   Getting excited helps a lot! But users still won't adopt something unless they see a need or have a strong want for it. Sometimes we don't know we need something until we see it. I never knew I needed a smart phone until I saw one in use, then I absolutely needed one. We must demonstrate the need for the change. The need might be regulatory, legal, increased productivity, time savings, financial savings, process improvement, or goal or mission alignment. Try to

demonstrate needs that directly benefit the person. Make it as self-serving for them as you can.

c. Confidence
Now you need or want the change and you're excited about it. But that will only go so far for adoption if you don't feel capable of doing what the change requires. Help build people's confidence in their ability to easily and quickly learn the new thing. You can do this by providing peer support, having peers who are more confident help support others in their learning process. Demonstrations, prototypes, and micro-learning are another great way to build confidence. Remember that people fear what they don't know. Once they get their hands on something and it becomes more tangible and less conceptual, their confidence will increase.

23. What is user adoption vs. user adaptability? And why do I care?

Adoption is the process of taking on something completely new. When we think of things that are genuinely new they are often world changing, like the microwave or indoor electricity or the telephone. Most of the time we are not creating something completely new. Sometimes we do, and when we do it's fantastic.

Adapting it adjusting to shifting conditions of things we already know. It's more likely that the projects we work on are taking something existing and changing it, improving upon it, adding features, changing a look, piecing different existing things together into something new. Take the smart watch for example. It takes pieces of things we already know; a wrist watch, touch screens, apps; and puts them together. It's not brand new. It is a compilation of things with which we're already familiar.

Why this distinction? I suggest that our change management plan should be different depending on if we're aiming for user adoption vs. user adaptability; if you're creating something completely new or if you're shifting and adapting already familiar things.

Question 20 addresses the principles of user adoption. The next two pages explain the principles of user adaptability.

Principles of User Adaptability

1. *Assume Change Saturation: Which means, dare I say it, we don't need to do a change tolerance assessment for user adaptability. We already know everybody is saturated with change.*

2. *Assume Expectations of Change: Thanks to people's interactions with technology in their personal lives, they have learned to expect change. Leverage that expectation. Let them start to expect it at work, too. If the change is small enough don't announce it, or give documentation, or train on it. Just do it. This idea only works if we also focus on principle #6.*

3. *Expectation Inflation (see question 26): Stakeholders will make assumptions or hold expectations that are not realistic to your project. Know it, name it. Try to ascertain what those expectations are so you can manage them down. Know that there are things that will be unstated which will be assumed to be included.*
(continued on next page)

Principles of User Adaptability

4. Deliver High Quality: This does not mean gold-plate. This means take pride in what you deliver and make sure the quality supports a simple and intuitive user experience.

5. Build Anticipation: Get people excited and wanting what's coming. Show them the advantages and how their lives will be easier. Remove fears, and offer pain killers. We want people to line up for the change. Think Apple Store the day a new iphone is released.

6. Objective of No Training Required: You might not get 100% there, but if you keep this objective as a goal, then you'll certainly get closer. This principle speaks to the quality of the user experience and will go a long way toward users adapting. This is also wonderfully selfish. Wouldn't it be awesome if you didn't have to spend any time training? Keep that selfish perspective and you'll approach things differently in a way that benefits everybody.

CHAPTER 4: SCOPE

Requirements are what the customer wants.

Scope is the work to be done.

24. What are some methods for gathering requirements?

This list of techniques comes from PMI's PMBOK® guide. The definitions for each technique are an abridged interpretation.

  a. Affinity Diagrams
     Take all the brainstorming ideas and classify them into groups.

  b. Benchmarking
     Find an organization similar to your own and look at what they're doing.

  c. Brainstorming
     Think of and write down all the ideas, without value judgments or prioritization.

  d. Context Diagrams
     A visual depiction of how users will use the thing. What they might put into it and what comes out of it.

  e. Document Analysis
     Got documentation? Read it.

  f. Facilitated Workshops & Focus Groups
     Facilitate a group of stakeholders and subject matter experts through an interactive conversation.

  g. Interviews
     This is likely the most popular method. Ask people lots of questions in person or over the phone.

h. Mind Mapping
Draw a visual map of how things connect. This could be process based or grouped by topic, team, or project phase.

i. Nominal Group Technique
Vote on and rank the ideas from your brainstorming session.

j. Observations
Watch people. But not in a creepy, stalking kind of way. Get their permission first and then watch what they do.

k. Prototypes
Create a smaller version or representation of the thing you're building.

l. Reverse Engineering
Take it apart, look at all the individual pieces, reassemble.

m. Surveys
Ask people lots of questions in writing.

25. While gathering requirements I noticed that some of them don't seem appropriate or helpful for the business objectives of the project. Some might even hurt the desired outcome. But these are the requirements provided by the customer. What should I do?

A) Do them anyway, and cry a little.
B) Follow your heart and do what you believe is right, but don't tell the stakeholders until the project is over. Surely they will thank you in the end.
C) Throw the project in the trash since it's doomed for failure.
D) Find a way to influence the stakeholders.

The correct answer is D, find a way to influence the stakeholders. The term "requirements gathering," can be a bit misleading. It sounds like your role is to passively collect information. As the project manager your role should be to help influence the overall direction of the project toward success. Sometimes this could mean actively helping to shape, refine, and define requirements.

You could use requirements gathering tools like mapping and prototyping to show stakeholders where things could be better. Actively offer up suggestions. Ask them to demonstrate how their requirements are supporting the business objective. Play an active role in facilitating group discussions, and help lead the stakeholders to more desirable outcomes by asking critical thinking questions around intent, impact, and what alternatives would look like. If you do it right, you can ask them questions that will shape their thinking in the direction you want it to go.

26. What is Expectation Inflation? And why do I care?

It starts with the fast paced world in which we live. Technology, driven by competition, continues to accelerate the pace of change, leaving us to adapt to changes or fall quickly and helplessly behind. Our quick adoption of new technologies, in particular in our personal lives, creates expectations about how we interact with technology in general. Combine that with the acceleration of the pace of change, and our expectations are continuously inflating.

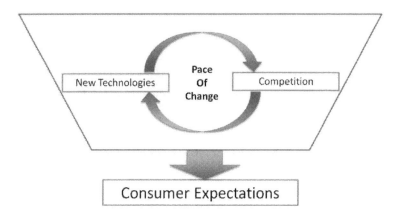

This expectation inflation results in something like the email on the next page.

The Midnight Email

Do you ever get messages like this from your boss, sent in the middle of the night, cryptic but clearly expecting something of you?

Date: 3/19/2016 12:04 AM

Subject: Can we do this?

http://www.worldofwatches.com/wowtv
Our new site will do this, right?

You've just experienced expectation inflation.

Expectation inflation is when stakeholders make assumptions or hold expectations that are not realistic to your project, influenced by their experiences with technology. You can think of it as the parent to scope creep, only this is worse because often it's an unspoken assumption. Ah, now you're starting to see why you care. People are holding assumptions about what you can accomplish and especially with what resources because, after all, they can tweet a pizza icon and get a pizza delivered to their door, so how hard could it possibly be to add that extra feature?

Examples:
    a. Seeing something new and assuming it is already included or at the least can be easily added onto your project.

    b. Somebody sees or uses a technology in their personal life and makes the "logical" leap that your company already does or should deliver similar capabilities with minimal or no additional resources or time.

27. How can I prevent scope creep?

With a waterfall method, using a change request process can be effective. Any change is logged, considered, given a time estimate and associated cost, and then approved or denied. With agile, change requests go into a backlog and are weighed and considered for a future iteration.

In reality, it's not always as straightforward as that. A great way to prevent or at least deter scope creep is to understand and demonstrate the complete impact of the change. This includes communicating the impact to time, budget, resources, and quality; but could also include things like impact to training, documentation, security, delays to other projects because of resource availability, and impact to morale.

The more you are able to show impact that carries with it a direct consequence to the person requesting the change, the more likely you are to stop the scope creep.

The Bigger They Are...

Picture a small car driving up a very steep road to get over a mountain. The small car can make it up and over with little to no difficultly. A bigger car will start to struggle as it gets closer to the top. A big truck will struggle the most, downshifting gears and pushing its engine to the max to make it over the crest.

Projects are the same. The bigger they are, the more resistance you'll face as you get closer to launching at the end, closer to reaching the summit of the tall mountain. Push through it, keep going, and don't let those who are challenging your project stop you now! Get that truck over the mountain!

28. People keep requesting specific project deliverables that require customization. Customizing is expensive, difficult to maintain, and creates risk. The more we can stick to an out-of-the-box solution the better off we'll be in the long term. How can I deter requests for customizations?

Customization requests are typically prevalent when working on a project to implement a new software. People like things done the way they've always done it, so they try to make the technology fit their current process rather than adapt their processes to fit the technology. As project managers we often find ourselves encouraging, pushing, or forcing people to adapt their processes in order to maintain the software implementation best practice of avoiding or limiting customizations.

A great way to manage requests for customizations is to create a **customization policy** at the beginning of the project. The policy should provide guidelines and requirements for determining if a customization is warranted. Any customization that comes up would then be run through the process outlined in the policy. An example is provided on the next page.

Sample Customization Policy

Best practice when leveraging a new software platform is to choose configuration over customization. Our company will adhere to these standards by applying the guidelines detailed below.

Customizations should not necessarily be required in order to meet the pre-existing business processes of the organization, no matter how culturally embedded they are. This is an opportunity to analyze those processes, reconcile them with the character of the organization, and alter or possibly eliminate them.

The following will be addressed when considering a process or business rule for customization:
1. Identify the business need.
2. What is the history of how and why it was established?
3. What will best effectively serve the character of the organization?
4. Is it necessary to effectively deliver mission-critical products and services?
5. What out-of-the-box alternatives are available?
6. Will any of the alternatives satisfy the identified business needs?
7. Weigh customization cost vs. benefit.

These standards have been established in order to account for the cost of customizations to the organization; in money, project time, and resources; and to weigh the long-term consequences of future upgrades.

CHAPTER 5: TIME

29. How can I provide a quick time estimate?

Consider how long you think it would take you to complete the task or project, your first instinct. Now double it. It's the x2 rule. If you think you can get something done in a week, estimate two weeks. Some people prefer the x3 rule.

30. How can I protect my project's timeline?

Set a good idea cutoff date.

Everybody has good ideas that they want included in your project. The ideas will keep coming, and with that are expectations that those ideas will happen. Set and communicate a good idea cutoff date, after which date the ideas will be saved for future iterations but won't make it into the scope of work you're currently executing. The SCRUM method is great at doing this with how it manages development sprints and backlogs new ideas. If you're not using SCRUM or other agile methods, then a having a good idea cutoff date is a great alternative.

31. **My project is behind schedule. I don't have extra resources to add and I've already paralleled all the tasks I can. The problem is that I'm waiting on people to give input or feedback and they are not responding in a timely manner because it's not a priority for them. I don't manage them so I can't adjust their priorities. What can I do?**

   1. Reset Expectations
   Any time your timeline is impacted, it's important to communicate that and to reset expectations around completion. If the timeline can't change, then other expectations would need to change such as resources needed, scope of work that can be completed within the timeline, or quality of the work that can be done within the timeline.

   2. Explain the Impact
   Write up the facts about the impact of the delay and communicate that directly to the people causing the delay. Writing it down first will help you to stick to just the facts and leave emotion out of it. Let them know how their delay is affecting other people and affecting themselves as a stakeholder. Try not to talk about the impact to yourself as that will come across as self-interested. The best is if you demonstrate the impact to the company, to people higher up, and to the persons directly.

   3. Understand the Competition
   What are the other things that are taking priority over your requests? Why are they taking priority? Has there been a change in resource availability? Or do people not see the impact or value of doing the work so they are self-prioritizing it as low?

4. Reexamine the Priority
   If stakeholders aren't prioritizing the work, then it might be time to reexamine how much of a priority it actually is. Maybe something changed that you don't know about. Talk with your PMO director, portfolio manager, or project sponsor about the prioritization.

5. Escalate
   Raise the issue to your project sponsor and let them determine when and how to raise the issue with the offender's manager.

32. What's a Critical Path? And why do I care?

A critical path is the longest sequence of activities that it takes to complete a project. It shows you the maximum duration that the project should take. If any activity on the critical path is not completed on schedule, the overall project timeline will be impacted.

If an activity can be completed without impacting the overall timeline (for example, parallel tasks) then it would not be considered part of the critical path.

Milestones should all be on the critical path.

If you monitor and analyze activities on the critical path and can uncover trends (e.g. is a certain person or particular activity type always late or early), you can *proactively* identify if a project is at risk of getting off track. It enables you to take proactive measures instead of reactive.

Never put off until tomorrow what you can do the day after tomorrow.

--Mark Twain

33. How can I manage my time better?

Here are a few ideas to try.
    a. Group meetings together back to back. It forces a hard stop since you would have to get to your next meeting. It also can eliminate the short 30-60 minute time slots that frequently occur in between meetings which are generally less productive as it's not enough time to get fully engaged in other work.

    b. Schedule your meetings in 25 or 50 minute blocks instead of 30 or 60 minutes. That way you have a few minutes at the end of a meeting to prep for your next meeting or take a personal comfort break.

    c. Block off work time on your calendar and name what that work time is for. Don't schedule over it. If you have to schedule over it, then make sure you can move your work time to another time so you don't lose it.

    d. Answer emails in time blocks. When working on other stuff, if possible, don't answer your email. You might glance at email to see if there is something urgent, but if the email is not urgent then read and respond later. If you end up with 30-60 minutes between meetings, you can use that time to respond to emails.

    e. Establish communication norms. For example: emails are for non-urgent messages that require more time to read and/or answer, chat or text is for more urgent or quick answer messages, phone calls are for urgent communications.

f. Know what time of day you're most productive and, if possible, adjust your schedule to work during those hours.

g. Start your day with a prioritized to-do list.

34. How can I have a better work/life balance, without quitting my job?

We're all seeking the answer to the elusive work/life balance mystery. In the words of the wise Kung Fu Panda, "There is no secret ingredient." Maybe right now you're having a similar reaction as Kung Fu Panda's enemy, Tai Lung, after he had been waiting to get the secret answer for so many years and finally got the magic scroll which held the answer. He opened it and saw it was blank. He declared in dismay, "It's nothing!"

"It's okay. I didn't get it the first time either," Po responded.

"What!?!" Tai Lung was upset to say the least.

"There is no secret ingredient. It's just you."

We all desperately want there to be a secret answer to work/life balance. In truth, the answer lies within each of us. We must each find our own path to work/life sustainability, the foundation of which is piecing together a combination of time management tips that works for you. This will be different for everybody. Some like to start their day writing up a list of tasks they want to accomplish. Some like to take regular ten minute breaks throughout the day. Some like to save up all their vacation days and take off two weeks, while some prefer to take one day off every two to three weeks. Work/life balance is the most personal and important time management that any of us do.

CHAPTER 6: RISK

35. What goes into a risk register?

There are a variety of risk register templates out there. They consistently include four areas or groupings with *key components. Additional components vary depending on usefulness to the project and the project manager's working style. Here is a list of items with some examples to consider including in your risk register.

1. Forecast
   - *ID / Risk number
   - *Type – threat or opportunity
   - *Identified risk – risk description and consequence
   - Root cause
   - Status – active, closed, critical
   - Project phase – initiation, planning, execution, design, configuration, testing, go-live, close out, post-live
   - Risk type – scope, budget, schedule, quality
   - Risk category – management, environment, project, technical, functional
   - Trigger – what will cause the risk to become a real issue
   - Effect – what happens when the risk is triggered, how quickly will the effect take place and to what impact

2. Quantitative Assessment
   - *Probability score (could go up to 5)
     - 1 – Low, unlikely to happen
     - 2 – Medium, may happen
     - 3 – High, likely to happen

   - *Impact score (could go up to 5)
     - 1 – Low, minimal disruption to project progress

- 2 – Medium, moderate disruption to project progress, threatens project vision, schedule implications, or reduces project benefits
- 3 – High, extended disruption to project progress, cost implications, threatens viability of project or represents project failure

- *Risk rating = probability x impact
  - 1-2 – Minor risks, recommended for more liberal response plans and occasional monitoring
  - 3-4 – Moderate risks, recommended for mid-range response plans (mitigate or transfer where possible), clearly defined actions plans and regular monitoring
  - 6-9 – Major risks, recommended for aggressive response plans, preferably avoidance, clearly defined action plans and frequent monitoring

3. Response Strategy / Action Plan
   - *Response strategy – how to respond to the risk *before* it happens: accept, avoid, mitigate, transfer, exploit, enhance, share
   - *Response plan – description of action to take *before* the risk happens
   - Trigger warning signs
   - *Contingency / action plan – how to respond if the risk becomes reality

4. Monitor and Control
   - *Owner
   - *Current status
   - *Status date / Date entered
   - Next review date
   - Date closed
   - *Comments

36. How frequently should a risk register be reviewed and updated?

A good general rule is every other week, but it's up to you to determine if you should review more or less frequently depending on the size and complexity of the project and on the volume and degree of risks. If you track a date for follow up in the risk register, set up a task reminder in your calendar to prompt you to review the risk on that date.

You should review risks during status meetings with your project sponsor. Your sponsor can provide additional insight that might change the quantitative rating, response plans, and when to review risks again. Setting the standard of reviewing risks with your sponsor also ensures that you have a set time to review risks.

37. What are some common project risks to include or consider in a risk register?

Risk Category	Risk Description
Management	- Complexity of decision making requirements and signoffs - Cultural speed of the organization - Lack of executive oversight, resulting in delays in critical decision making, unclear project status understanding, and ineffective risk mitigation actions
Project	- Users do not agree on project goals, requirements, or priorities - Consider whether the customer expectations and success criteria are clearly defined and understood - Consider the extent to which project scope is clearly defined, understood, documented, or extremely complex - Consider the extent to which the project schedule contains sufficient time to complete the project
Functional	- Users don't understand or can't describe their own business processes or requirements - Consider the amount and complexity of processes and policy changes required - Likelihood the solution will require extensive complex testing, or that planned or actual testing effort may be inadequate

Risk Category	Risk Description
Environment	- Dependencies on other projects or systems
- Availability, commitment, and knowledge of users
- Complexity of organizational or team structures
- Likelihood of key personnel leaving
- Likelihood of organizational priorities shifting
- Likelihood the business benefits of the project have not been clearly documented, communicated to, or recognized by project stakeholders
- Likelihood that the customer does not realize or understand the support requirements for the new solution
Technical	- Availability of appropriate technically skilled, experienced people from partner team(s)
- Current availability of compliant hardware and infrastructure, including test space
- Likelihood of customizations requested during the project
- Likelihood that the project will require integration with other applications
- Consider whether the project will include any unproven or pre-beta versions of software products

Assumptions are a project's worst enemy.

38. What makes an assumption so dangerous?

An assumption is an existing belief that a thing is true. Whether it is actually true or not, we believe that it is. What makes those beliefs particularly risky in the workplace is the combination of three distinguishing characteristics of assumptions.

- a. We believe them to be true when they might not be.

- b. We make decisions and take actions based on assumptions.

- c. We don't usually think to communicate them.

39. Assumptions introduce a lot of risk. What are some common assumptions to watch out for?

1. Assuming a project or task is easier or faster than it actually is.
    Could lead to scope creep, a lot of change requests, and unrealistic expectations on timeline.

2. Assuming we already know the solution to our problem.
    Could lead to asking for solutions instead of communicating the problem, giving someone an easy out to say no to your proposed solution, limiting creative problem solving and partnership, and banging your head against your desk.

3. Assuming priorities are aligned and haven't changed.
    Could lead to projects losing sponsorship, losing resources, timeline delays, and crying.

4. Assuming oho owns, or is responsible for, what.
    Could lead to communication breakdowns, tasks not getting done, blaming others instead of solving problems, negative feelings, impact on user adoption, and watching cat videos.

5. Assuming people don't know how use technology.
    Could lead to creating processes for exceptions.

6. Assuming we know all the implications of changes we make.
    Could lead to complete and utter disaster.

40. How can I uncover assumptions people might be holding that would impact my work?

You can't stop assumptions from happening, but you can uncover them to mitigate the risks assumptions might create.

- a. Explore your own assumptions.
  Write down what assumptions you're holding. Really think about things you're taking for granted and put it in writing.

- b. Share your assumptions.
  Share what you wrote with your key stakeholders. By checking your own assumptions, you will learn which of your assumptions were wrong and need adjusting. It will also get other people thinking about their own assumptions and hopefully sharing and checking theirs.

- c. Ask lots of questions.
  Why am I asking questions? Do you think it will help me learn about assumptions? Is this really going to work? How do I know it is working? What kind of questions should I ask? Is modeling asking questions working?

- d. Ask people for a list of their questions.
  One possible way to uncover assumptions people are holding is through the questions they ask, and the questions they don't ask. For example, if your timeline is tight and they don't ask anything about timing then they are most likely holding some assumptions about the feasibility of your timeline that might not be true.

e. Ask people what other people are saying. "Did Rashad talk with you about <insert important thing>? How did he explain it to you? What questions did he ask you? What was his take on it, how does he understand it?"

f. Checking Assumptions Exercise.
Create a collaborative spreadsheet and ask your team and/or key project contributors to write down their assumptions about a project. Then have each person score everyone else's assumptions, don't score your own:
    -1 if you were unaware of the assumption
    0 if you independently held the same assumption
    +1 if you already knew of that person's assumption

Sum up the scores. Look at the assumptions with the lowest values. Have a conversation about those and see if you've uncovered new risks to consider.

Another way to use this exercise is to ask people to write their assumptions about how you work together as a team, to help shape a more deliberate team culture or to foster better collaboration.

This exercise also works well for aligning expectations. Instead of writing down assumptions, write down expectations. See examples on the following pages.

Checking Assumptions Exercise

Name	Assumptions	Scores				How We Did
		[Person1]	[Person2]	[Person3]	[Person4]	
[Person1]		----				0
		----				0
		----				0
[Person2]			----			0
			----			0
			----			0
[Person3]				----		0
				----		0
				----		0
[Person4]					----	0
					----	0
					----	0

Scoring: -1 if you were unaware of the assumption
0 if you independently held the same assumption
+1 if you already knew of that person's assumption

Aligning Expectations Exercise

Name	Expectations	Scores				How We Did
		[Person1]	[Person2]	[Person3]	[Person4]	
[Person1]		----				0
		----				0
		----				0
[Person2]			----			0
			----			0
			----			0
[Person3]				----		0
				----		0
				----		0
[Person4]					----	0
					----	0
					----	0

Scoring: -1 if you were unaware of the expectation
+1 if you already knew of that person's expectation
+2 if you independently held the same expectation

Risk Management is a Mindset

Risk management is more of a mindset than a spreadsheet. Documenting risks is a good way to force time to deliberately think about risks, to include input from others in the process, and serves as a reminder of what to keep an eye on throughout a project. But risk management so much more than that. It's a mindset of constantly thinking about and employing mitigation.

You know you have a mindset for risk if...
- *you factor risks into most of your decision-making processes*
- *it comes up in a lot of your conversations*
- *you frequently encourage others to think about risk*
- *you inquire about what actions are being taken to reduce risk*
- *your vacations have mitigation plans*

CHAPTER 7: PROCESS

The SAM Approach

This approach is applicable to a wide variety of processes. It is a useful framework for everything from implementing software to starting up a new business.

Solidify – Build the core
Get a structure set up and working. Focus on the minimal viable product (MVP). Keep what works and get rid of what doesn't.

Amplify – Increase the impact
Add more features and functions. Improve the user experience. Start to see ROI, better inform decisions and goals, and realize greater value.

Multiply – Expand usage
Scale the work such that you're having a broader reach with more impact using the same or fewer resources.

41. How can I tell if a project is getting off track before it's too late?

The key is to identify trends.

   a. Look at your timeline milestones. Have you reached them on time? Is there a trend in being late? Does it look like you might miss one that's coming up soon?

   b. Look at your budget. If your current rate of spending stays consistent, will you be over budget? Are there any big expenses coming up soon? Have there been repeated unplanned expenses or asks for additional money?

   c. Look at your scope. Have there been a lot of requests for changes to scope?

   d. Talk to stakeholders about how they feel the project is going. Do they have concerns that need to be addressed?

It is human nature to ask for a solution rather than to explain the problem.

July 2015, my son was four and a half years old. One night when he was in bed he called me saying, "Mommy, I'm hot." I replied, "Okay, I'll go turn down the air." Next night he said again, "Mommy, I'm hot." I said, "I'll turn down the air."

On the third night he said, "Mommy, can you turn down the air?" It just so happened that night, unlike the other nights, I had covered him up with blankets and had already turned down the air. The solution on that night was to take off the blankets. When I saw my four-year-old ask for a solution, that's when I realized how ingrained it is in our very nature to ask for solutions rather than explain the problem.

When Seeking Help Present Problems, Not Solutions

If you're asking someone to help solve a problem, always present the problem itself and not what you think the solution should be. It will result in more creative problem solving. Presenting the solution gives the other person an easy out to say they can't do that and move on. Presenting the problem forces the other person to think of solutions that would work.

If you're presented a solution to execute, always ask what the problem is that you're solving. You'll get better results since their assumptions on a solution might be incorrect or misinformed. They might be asking for the air to be turned down when they need to take off the blanket.

Never create processes for exceptions.

Let's Not

I was in a team meeting discussing a website built primarily for mobile devices. One page was designed for landscape, horizontal viewing, and the other pages were built vertical portrait. The team, including myself, was concerned about this difference and one person suggested we add instructions telling users to turn their mobile device. Wait. What? Do we really think people don't know to turn their mobile device if the screen changes direction?

This is an easy trap to fall into. We make assumptions about people's capabilities to execute simple tasks. Those assumptions result in creating processes for every possible scenario, including exceptions. The more branches we add to a process tree, the more complicated we make things for both ourselves and the end users and the more it impacts user adoption. A simple experience will increase user adoption. As we look at project requirements we should ask, "What is the simplest solution? What are the minimal requirements to achieve the business objective?" We should watch for processes built to exceptions and say, "let's not."

42. What's the difference between Waterfall and Agile?

With a waterfall, water starts at the top and flows down. It goes in one direction. Similarly, the project steps go in one direction through the project phases of initiating, planning, executing while monitoring and controlling, and closing. In reality it's not so one-directional, but the idea is that the processes flow, for the most part, in one direction.

Agile is a philosophy on how a project can be approached. At its core is the idea of iterations, or working in cycles. So rather than flowing in one direction, it flows more circular. Get requirements, plan, execute, release to client and test, repeat. Agile methods are popular with software and technology development.

A hybrid approach (Watergile? Agfall? ...still working on a name) is becoming more popular as project managers see the benefits of both methods, pick out the parts that work for them, and piece it together. Some favorite principles from Agile are testing and having feedback loops throughout the project rather than at the end, and collecting user stories to define requirements. Some favorites from Waterfall are using milestones to track the project timeline, and having documented project plans.

43. What is the Agile Manifesto?

We value:

    Individuals and interactions over processes and tools

    Working software over comprehensive documentation

    Customer collaboration over contract negotiation

    Responding to change over following a plan

That is, while there is value in the items on the right, we value the items on the left more.

44. What is this thing called SCRUM? It sounds silly.

SCRUM is an agile method, and not silly at all. It's an iterative development process used primarily in software development. The main features of a SCRUM process include:

    a. A backlog of features to develop.

    b. Picking from the backlog what features will be developed during a defined time period called a sprint. The length of a development sprint can vary, but is typically around thirty days. Once a sprint is started, any new feature requests would go to the backlog and not be included in that development cycle. New requests could be considered for a future sprint.

    c. During a sprint, holding daily stand up meetings. The team literally stands up at the start of each day and each person says:
        1. What they've done since the last stand-up meeting
        2. What they plan to do before the next one
        3. Issues with which they need help to resolve

    d. Roll out new functionality

    e. Repeat

45. What's the difference between process management, project management, and product management?

Why do you have a manager? What does that manager do for you in managing your work? Perhaps they help assign and prioritize your work. They hold you accountable for getting your work completed on time and for the quality of your work. Your manager might coach or train you, help answer questions and give you advice. They make sure your work aligns with your company's business objectives, that you are working on the right things. Your manager (hopefully) makes sure you develop and grow professionally.

Now take those same management principles, and whatever others you've thought of, and apply them to a process, project, or product.

A process is a series of actions or steps taken in order to achieve a particular end. It's a repeatable sequence of tasks without uniqueness and no clearly defined end state.

A project is a temporary endeavor undertaken to create a unique product, service, or result. A project has a distinct start and end. When a project is over the project manager walks away and moves on to the next project.

A product is a thing that is manufactured or refined for sale. Products spend most of their life in maintenance. A product manager stays with the product and continues to manage the product throughout its life.

CHAPTER 8: PORTFOLIOS

46. What is portfolio management?

In the words (mostly) of PMI:
Portfolio management includes the process of evaluating, selecting, and prioritizing a group of projects. It requires using a strategic lens to ensure alignment with organizational strategies and goals. It also includes allocating resources and demonstrating measurable impact. A significant benefit of portfolio management is that it enables organizations to optimize resources in support of the most strategically significant projects and programs.

In my words:
Do you have more project requests than you can possibly complete with your current resources? You have to pick what to work on first, what waits, and what doesn't get done at all. And you want the greatest impact for the resources invested. It's time to estimate, evaluate, allocate, and prioritize. Portfolio management to the rescue.

47. What process could I use to evaluate project requests?

1. Understand the Why
   First get at the reason why the project request was made, without making judgements. Be sure to check all your assumptions.
   a. Ask questions until you clearly understand the business case, the impact of the project. You can start by asking for their written business case. Then follow up with a lot of questions.
   b. Listen and demonstrate your understanding of and empathy for the requestor's pain and needs.
   c. If it makes sense to do so, suggest alternative solutions to meet the core need.

2. Consider Connections
   Ask around to other people to get informed answers to the following questions. Again, be sure to check all your assumptions.
   a. Connect to People – Could this benefit other staff? Would this require help or time from other staff?
   b. Connect to Strategy – Does this align with your team's and company's strategic goals?
   c. Connect to Systems – Does this have significant impact on connected systems or processes?

48. What criteria could I use to prioritize projects?

The criteria should be directly linked to your company's and team's strategic goals and mission. Here are some generic prioritization criteria:

a. Is it a pain killer or a vitamin? In other words, will the project outcome take away something painful, or is it a value-add?
b. Where is the greatest gap?
c. Which will have the widest usage across departments, staff, and customers?
d. Does it enable staff and customer growth?
e. Does it create something that doesn't exist, or does it take an existing thing from good to great?
f. External and internal driving deadlines.
g. Bandwidth of the project team.

What other criteria do you use?

_____

_____

_____

_____

49. How can I tell people that we won't work on their project when they want it, or possibly not at all, without ruining my relationship with them?

Understand the problem that the project was aiming to solve.
    Communicate your understanding of their situation. Express empathy and really try to put yourself in their shoes.

Provide context.
    Explain your process and selection criteria. Share what the competing projects are that pushed theirs back or out, and the impact of those projects. Providing context will help develop an understanding on their side.

If possible, let them pick.
    If two stakeholders are in competition for getting their projects completed, try facilitating a conversation between the two of them with a goal of having them decide which project should be worked on first. Start the conversation by explaining why the available resources won't allow you to do both projects at the same time, and tell them you're seeking their advice and input.

If possible, suggest some alternatives or partial solutions that might be faster, cheaper, or they can do on their own.
    By suggesting alternatives, you are demonstrating that you want to help even if you can't do everything they are asking for in the timeline they've requested.

CHAPTER 9: TEAMS

> *Tell me how you measure me and I will tell you how I will behave. If you measure me in an illogical way, do not complain about illogical behavior.*
>
> *--Eli Goldratt*

50. What are some tips on leading a virtual team?

1. Use metrics. It's harder to "see" what someone is working on since you can't walk by their desk. Find ways to measure their work to ensure they are on track.

2. Schedule a weekly (at a minimum) recurring check-in meeting with each team member, and set a standard of turning on your video cameras.

3. Chat or email a random, "hello, how was your weekend?" or, "anything fun happening today?" Be deliberate about building relationships and checking in on your team to see how things are going outside of scheduled meetings.

4. Send a funny YouTube video just to make them laugh. Humor helps develop relationships.

5. Provide regular and thorough feedback. Set aside specific times to talk just about performance. At the end of the conversation ask the person to write up what they got out of it and email a summary to you. That will allow you to check for alignment.

6. Use online collaborative documents and spreadsheets that can be opened and edited by multiple people at the same time.

7. Use an online project management or task tracking tool. See question 58 for some project management tools.

8. Hold your team meetings via video conference, not just on the phone. Turn on your cameras. See question 60 for some conferencing tools.

51. How can I make my team meetings more productive?

1. Assign a facilitator and rotate who facilitates.

2. Start the meeting with a quick ice breaker, typically a fun question where you learn something about each other. Or start with shout-outs where anybody on the team can recognize someone for great work or excellent collaboration.

3. Have an agenda.

4. Have everyone on the team contribute to the agenda. Circulate an agenda template at least a day in advance and have the team fill out ahead of time what they're working on and items for discussion.

5. Spend the first part of the meeting having each person give a quick update on what they're working. Keep it short, two minutes per person.

6. Have the rest of the meeting open for discussion items, important updates, announcements and reminders.

7. Take time to celebrate wins. Have someone tell a story of the win. Use pictures, if appropriate, to help tell the story.

52. What is a team promise and why should I have one?

A team promise is a written document that defines your team culture by stating how you promise to work with each other. It serves as a way to explicitly call out assumptions on behavioral expectations, and is a way to hold each other accountable.

A team promise works best when written together as a team and reviewed between two to four times a year as a team. The promise is a living document, meaning that it can change. Your team and/or working environment will change so the team promise should change with it.

Here are some examples of things that could go into a team promise:

a. We are honest with each other, and give/take feedback with generosity of spirit.
b. We are open to one another's perspective.
c. We share in our successes and shortcomings.
d. We own our mistakes as well as congratulate one another on our successes.
e. We value wellness (personal and professional health) and support the team during one another's time off.
f. We are interested in each other personally, and are comfortable asserting personal boundaries.
g. We are respectful of different working styles, roles, and project ownership.
h. It is safe to disagree amongst ourselves. We are united externally.
i. When frustrated, focus on the situation to support a solution-oriented mindset rather than blaming a person.

What would you like to see in your team promise?

_____

_____

_____

_____

53. What are some good, quick team building activities and icebreakers?

Here are some that can be done virtually or in-person:
   a. Two Truths and a Lie. Each person tells two truths and one lie, and others have to guess which the lie is.
   b. What's in Your Bag or What's on Your Desk. Have each person show (on video if virtual) and talk about one thing that's in their bag, or one thing that's on their desk.
   c. If you could travel to any fictional location, where would you go and why?
   d. If you could travel to any time, past or future, what time would you travel to and why?
   e. What's your guilty pleasure?
   f. Share a favorite holiday tradition, past or present.
   g. Share a favorite quote or saying.
   h. What is a decision you made that changed the trajectory of your life?

Here are a few for in-person groups only:
   a. The Game of Possibilities
      Materials: Cloth napkins. Instructions: Divide into groups. Give a napkin to each group. One person at a time has 15 seconds to demonstrate a use for the napkin. The person demonstrating cannot speak. The demonstration must be original. Go around until one group can't come up with anything.

   b. Speed Dating
      Materials: Everybody needs a sheet of paper and pen. Write everybody's name on the paper. Instructions: Pair off, set a timer and switch every two minutes. You get two minutes with each person to identify and write down as many things as you can that you

have in common with each other. Do not count physical traits like eye or hair color. The person with the most things on their sheet wins.

   c. Concentration
      Materials: None. Instructions: Participants will need to form two equal lines facing each other. The game starts when one line turns around, giving the second line 40 seconds to change 10 things about themselves. This can include anything from jewelry or clothing being swapped with other people, untied shoelaces, a different hairdo, or a switched watch or ring to the other hand. All changes must be something the other group can see. After 40 seconds, the first group turns around and tries to find all the changes the other group made. Once the changes have been recognized, the groups switch, giving each team a chance to make changes. The team who spots the most changes correctly is the winner.

   d. How Observant Are You?
      Materials: Envelopes with instructions inside. Instructions: Divide into teams. Ask the teams to go to different locations so they can't see each other. Give each team an envelope that reads on the outside, "Set a timer for 5 minutes and start the timer when someone opens this envelope. Stop when the timer is up." The instructions inside read, "Write down as much as you can about what the other team is wearing. The team to get the most items correct wins."

54. How can I keep my team motivated, and avoid burn out for myself and my team?

1. Ensure there is variety in the work assigned and opportunities for creativity. Boredom is the enemy.

2. Plan time off well in advance, and include it in your project schedule.

3. Have fun and keep a sense of humor. That doesn't mean don't act professional. Where appropriate, and especially in the toughest of times, find something to laugh about.

4. Remind each other why you're doing this. It's easy to get caught up in the details and forget the bigger impact of the work.

5. Celebrate successes both big and small.

6. Show appreciation in little ways, like a simple private note, a shout-out to colleagues, or a Starbucks run.

How NOT to Give Feedback

I was standing in line at a Starbucks in Seattle and overheard a conversation between a woman and a man in front of me. The woman said, "I have some feedback for you."

The man replied with a concerned look on his face, "Oh no."

"Don't worry," she said, "its good feedback, not bad." She then proceeded to give the man some bad feedback. In public, no less.

Never pretend like you're about to say something positive to someone and then surprise them with something negative. If you have to give hard feedback, start by telling them that you need to have a direct conversation. Be honest and don't set any traps. And by all means, do not give negative feedback in public!

55. I have to give someone some hard feedback. What should I consider before going into the conversation?

1. Check any frustrations you have at the door.
2. Start with what you see, just the facts. Then ask their perception of what happened.
3. Listen with empathy. Know that there are always multiple sides to a story and that truth lives in the middle.
4. There is often a difference between intent behind words or actions and perception of those words or actions. Keep that in mind and call it out so the person hears that you understand their intent is likely different than how it was perceived, that you know they don't have bad intent. Once you both agree on the intent, then you can focus on how it was perceived and the real impact it had.
5. Share what behaviors you want to see. List skills you want them to develop.
6. Some who are conflict averse will forget what is said immediately after leaving the room. Give them something written to walk away with. Allow for processing time.
7. At the end, ask what they want from you. Schedule time to follow up and ask what they are walking away with.

Best advice I ever got regarding giving feedback, "Use lots of air quotes."

56. How do I start a conversation in which I'm giving hard feedback?

It's normal and natural to be nervous or fumble over your words when initiating a difficult conversation. Here are a few ways you could begin.

   a. "I'm not sure how to start this conversation, but it's important to have."

   b. "I would like for us to talk openly and honestly with each other about some important and difficult things."

   c. "Yesterday when you said, '(fill in the blank),' where did that come from?" Then listen with an open mind.

   d. "I've noticed some patterns of behavior that I'd like for us to talk through and see if we can uncover some root causes together."

57. How can I coach someone who needs to deliver hard feedback but is resistant because it makes them uncomfortable?

Here is some advice for managers who need to initiate hard conversations, but might be hesitating or struggling.

Don't trade off a moment of discomfort for weeks, months, or years of dealing with poor work. The longer you wait, the more you are hurting yourself as well as the other person. The closer you have the conversation to the time that the behaviors were observed, the more effective the conversation can be as it will seem more relevant.

Indecision is a decision. If you do nothing, then you've chosen by default to live with the behavior. It is your responsibility as a manger to say something, to point out what needs to change. Then it is up to the other person to change. But you can't expect them to change until you tell them the change you want to see.

CHAPTER 10: TOOLS

58. My project tracking needs have grown beyond Microsoft Excel. What are some good project management tools?

*Check out some of these great tools to see if they fit your needs:

a. AgileCraft.com – agile management
b. Asana.com – list based
c. Basecamp.com – list based
d. Celoxis.com – more robust
e. Clarizen.com – Gantt chart, for PMs, IT, and agile
f. Dapulse.com – visual, clean interface
g. Digite.com – card based; visual; more robust
h. Huddle.com – looks like a CRM
i. Leankit.com – card based; visual
j. LiquidPlanner.com – more robust
k. Meistertask.com – card based; visual
l. Microsoft Project – Gantt chart, more robust
m. Targetprocess.com – visual, scrum, kanban
n. Trello.com – card based
o. Workfront.com – for marketing, IT, and services teams
p. Wrike.com – Gantt chart, collaborative, for PMs and marketing

*this is not an endorsement

59. I need to track a portfolio of projects and resources. What are some portfolio and resource management tools?

*Some more tools worth looking into:

    a. 10000ft.com
    b. Celoxis.com
    c. Float.com
    d. Meisterplan.com
    e. Microsoft Project, it does portfolio tracking too
    f. Oracle Primavera
    g. PDWare.com
    h. Smartsheet.com
    i. Versionone.com – for agile project and portfolio management

*this is not an endorsement

60. What are other technology tools that could help me as a project manager?

*Many of these tools are great for scheduling and holding meetings, requirements gathering, training, user adoption, getting feedback, diagraming processes, and creating models and visualizations.

Appointment Scheduling
1. Doodle.com
2. ScheduleOnce.com
3. TimeCenter.com
4. Timetrade.com

Online Meetings & Screen Sharing
5. Adobe Connect
6. Hangouts.google.com
7. Join.me
8. Screenleap.com
9. Uberconference.com
10. Webex.com
11. Yugma.com (for Skype)

Document Sharing
12. Box.com
13. Dropbox.com
14. Google.com/drive
15. OneDrive.live.com

Notes and Checklists
16. Any.do
17. Evernote.com
18. GetPocket.com
19. Keep.google.com
20. Wunderlist.com

*this is not an endorsement

Mindmaps
21. Bubbl.us
22. Coggle.it
23. Matchware.com
24. Mindjet.com
25. Mindmeister.com
26. MindNode.com
27. XMind.net

Animation
47. Animaker.com
48. GoAnimate.com
49. MakeWebVideo.com
50. Powtoon.com

Online Whiteboard
28. Awwapp.com
29. RealtimeBoard.com
30. ScribLink.com
31. Ziteboard.com

Polls / Surveys
32. EasyPolls.net
33. KeySurvey.com
34. Polleverywhere.com
35. Qualtrics.com
36. Surveymonkey.com

Flowcharts / Diagrams
37. Creately.com
38. Draw.io
39. Gliffy.com
40. Lucidchart.com
41. Microsoft Visio

Infographics
42. Easel.ly
43. Infogr.am
44. Piktochart.com
45. Venngage.com
46. Vizualize.me

*still not an endorsement

CHAPTER 11: VENDORS

61. What are different types of requests sent to vendors?

RFP – Request for Proposal or Request for Partnership
- Proposal – solicits a bid for work. Typically includes info about the company who is making the request, detailed requirements, timeline expectations, and next steps with dates.

- Partnership – a new way of looking at an RFP. Instead of presenting the detailed requirements, the problem is presented in order to seek out a creative, problem-solving vendor to partner with in finding solutions.

RFQ – Request for Quote or Request for Qualifications
- Quote – solicits a bid from suppliers on a specific service or product.

- Qualifications – typically precedes a request for proposal and helps narrow down the list of vendors to send the proposal.

RFI – Request for Information
- A process to collect written information about the capabilities of business suppliers, frequently used in the construction industry.

62. Is there an alternative to a Request for Proposal (RFP)?

I'm so glad you asked. Yes! Some vendors who do excellent work won't respond to RFP's, and you don't want to miss out on opportunities for an amazing partnership with a great vendor. Sometimes all you need is something simpler like a request for quote in order to get the best bid, and sometimes your job requires RFP's due to the size and cost of the work. But if you're able to influence the process, here's a vendor selection method you can use as an alternative to sending out RFPs. Your vendors will thank you, your boss will thank you, and you will thank yourself.

a. Research online. A company's website says a lot about them.

b. Social source information. Ask on message boards in online communities for recommendations. Ask your networks and colleagues.

c. Narrow down to your top three to four. Reach out and schedule a call. Review high level requirements on the call.

d. Schedule demonstrations. In preparation:
   i. Provide the vendor with an outline of what you want to see. That way they will spend the demo time showing you the most relevant features. Don't have them show you a generic demo. An indicator of a good vendor is how well they stick to your outline.
   ii. Invite one to three key stakeholders to sit in on the demo. Limit the number of

people you invite, but make sure it's the same group of people on each demo.

    iii. Provide the stakeholders a scorecard (weighted if applicable) of project requirements and other factors such as customer service and technical expertise. Ask them to rate each item during the demo and send you their scorecards after each demo.

e. Evaluate the scorecards. Schedule any follow-up conversations to answer remaining questions. If you haven't found a vendor that satisfies your requirements, start back at step one.

f. Once you've narrowed it down to your top pick, go visit their office. You'll get a sense of their culture and working style. See if it fits yours. Culture fit is an important factor in understanding if the relationship is a good match. Visiting their office also demonstrates your commitment.

g. The Pre-Nup. Now you're ready to enter contract negotiation. Remind the vendor that it's the necessary predecessor to your marriage, but it doesn't mean you love them any less. Expect contract negotiations to take between two to three weeks if you need to involve legal counsel.

h. Congratulations! You've entered a beautiful new relationship that will last for years to come!

63. How can I foster a positive working partnership with a vendor?

One word. Transparency.

Tell the vendor truthfully what's going on with you and your company. Don't hide anything. Share what you're going through, what pressures you're under on your end, and ask your vendor what other pressures or competing priorities they have on their end in addition to the asks from your company. In the words of the wise PM Jedi Knight, "Transparency leads to trust. Trust leads to empathy. Empathy leads to cooperation."

64. How is vendor management changing? What trends should I be aware of?

Back in the day, like four years ago (that's ten "technology years"), we would seek out that one big software solution that solved twenty-five of our problems; and find the vendor to support, train, and customize that large solution. Now we buy twenty different small solutions, cloud based, self-trained, with no long-term commitment. The internet of things, connectedness of platforms, makes this approach possible.

Software selection has become more self-service, similar to personal shopping experiences in many ways. We do our own research first, ask our friends what they like (social sourcing of information), check out websites to compare the competition, do price-matching and search for coupons, and then complete the purchase through a self-service check-out line.

This has created a split in the kinds of vendors we partner with, ones who sell software and ones who sell services. Sometimes a vendor will do both, but that's becoming increasingly rarer. This shift is due to in part to software being designed with the idea of no training required. Vendors build something great with an excellent user experience, and there is little to no need for vendor support. They can focus more of their time on building, and we get to reap the rewards of an intuitive product.

The advantage to this approach is that it's more agile, responsive to change, easier to keep up with constantly shifting technology trends, allows for support of different working styles, easier to get user adoption, and can be more cost effective and financially predictable. The big risk to watch out for is data security. It's manageable if you're mindful of it, but you definitely have to pay more attention to security as multiple platforms are more connected.

This is one of the big shifting trends on how we interact with vendors, going from fewer vendors who offer more support on bigger platforms, to many vendors whose software requires less support while providing more flexibility. And in this constantly changing world of ours, who doesn't need more flexibility?

65. Things are taking a turn for the worse with a vendor that is critical to my project. What can I do?

Ask the "bad cop," aka your project sponsor, to step in.

> You need to maintain good relations with the vendor. It is the role of the project sponsor to push back and be the bad guy when needed. It's not that you aren't capable of pushing on vendors. It's that you shouldn't, because you need to have a different working relationship with them.

Use transparency and context to create empathy.

> Ask your vendor contact what's going on at their company, and if there is anything you can do to help. Show them empathy. Tell them what's going on with you, explain any pressures and why they are happening, and if there are other demands on you outside of the project the vendor is supporting. Provide context. It will help to create empathy. Often there are things outside of the project that is impacting you or the vendor. It helps to share those things and then see how you can find solutions together. And the more context you provide and the more transparent you are, the more likely you'll be to find solutions that work for everybody and your relationship will be stronger.

Problems always seem harder to solve when they are your own.

Contact the Author

www.bethspriggs.com

contact@bethspriggs.com

www.linkedin.com/in/bethspriggs
twitter @SpriggsBeth

Made in the USA
Columbia, SC
29 June 2017